Delicious Hullabaloo

Pachanga deliciosa

By/Por Pat Mora

Illustrations by/Ilustraciones por Francisco X. Mora

Spanish translation by/Traducción al español por
Alba Nora Martínez and Pat Mora

Piñata Books • Arte Público Press • Houston, Texas • 1998

Publication of *Delicious Hullabaloo* is made possible through support from the Andrew W. Mellon Foundation and the National Endowment for the Arts. We are grateful for their support.

Esta edición de *Pachanga deliciosa* ha sido subvencionada por la Fundación Andrew W. Mellon y el Fondo Nacional para las Artes. Les agradecemos su apoyo.

Piñata Books are full of surprises!

Piñata Books
An Imprint of Arte Público Press
University of Houston
Houston, Texas 77204-2174

Mora, Pat.
    Delicious Hullabaloo = Pachanga deliciosa / by Pat Mora; illustrations by Francisco X. Mora: Spanish translation by Alba Nora Martínez and Pat Mora.
        p.   cm.
    English and Spanish.
    Summary: In this poem in English and Spanish, lizards, armadillos, and other creatures of the night make merry beneath the desert moon, enjoying the strains of a mariachi band and gobbling lots of delicious food.
    ISBN 1-55885-246-8 (hbk. : alk. paper). — ISBN 1-55885-247-6 (pbk. : alk. paper)
    1. Children's poetry. American — Translations into Spanish. 2. Desert animals — Juvenile poetry. [1. Desert animals — Poetry materials — Bilingual.] I. Mora, Francisco X., ill. II. Title.
PS3563.073D45 1998   98-15532
811'.54—dc21   CIP
                                                           AC

For my nephew,
Christopher Mora Henry, who savors family.

Para mi sobrino, Christopher Mora Henry,
quien saborea familia.

P. M.

To all the children:
Little, big, white, red, brown, black, yellow, and blue.

Para todos niños:
Chiquitos, grandes, blancos, rojos, bronceados, negros, amarillos y azules.

F. X. M.

Hear the music

from moon and starlight?

Quick! Call our *amigos*

to bring their appetite.

¿Oyen la música

de la luna y las estrellas brillar?

¡Pronto! Llamen a nuestros amigos

que vengan a disfrutar.

Umm, smell the mangoes

calling this hot evening?

Hungry *lagartijas,*

we'll gobble anything.

¡Qué rico! ¿Huelen los mangos

esta tibia noche llamando?

Somos las lagartijas comelonas,

cualquier cosa devorando.

Here come the musicians

ready to pluck and play

música so juicy

we'll soon start to sway.

Allí vienen los músicos

listos para toque-tocar

música tan jugosa

ya empezaremos a bailar.

When lizards hear music
streaming from starlight,
they call, "Come, *amigos,*
join us on this orange night."

Al oír la música
brillante de las estrellas,
las lagartijas dicen, "Vengan,
amigos, a nuestra noche naranja."

"Cerezas dulces,"

pajarita sings,

"mouthfuls of red roundness

for our fiesta evening."

"Cerezas dulces,"

la pajarita canta,

"rojos bocados redondos

para la noche de fiesta."

Lizards stir tasty dishes,

toss tomatoes, cilantro, chiles too.

Lizards plot and plan

our delicious hullabaloo.

Las lagartijas mezclan tomates,

cilantro y chiles. ¡Qué mezcla sabrosa!

Las lagartijas planean y preparan

nuestra pachanga deliciosa.

Such mashing and smashing

by armadillo gourmet,

the sassy *salsa* splashing

as the musicians play.

Tal chaca y machaca

del gourmet armadillo,

la sabrosa salsa salpica

como los músicos con su cantadillo.

Armfuls of color
armadillos bring,
sashaying to the music
of plinging guitar strings.

Abrazando los colores
los armadillos se balancean,
al son de la música
que las guitarras rasguean.

Bees buzz ripe fruit.

Birds bring blooms to strew,

setting the table

for the hullabaloo.

Las abejas zumban la fruta.

Los pájaros ponen la mesa

que adornan con las flores

preparando la pachanga.

Mouthfuls of flavors,

such smacking, such glee

at savoring an evening

with friends and family.

Bocados de sabores,

tal gusto, tal felicidad,

al disfrutar una noche

en familia y amistad.

Armadillos, pour juices!

Lagartijas, sing with zest!

Amigos, tonight we'll swing

without any sleepiness.

Armadillos, ¡sirvan los jugos!

Lagartijas, ¡con gusto, a cantar!

Amigos, esta noche, todos

bailaremos sin descansar.

To friend fish, bird chatters

of trips she plans to take

across the sandy desert

on some yellow daybreak.

Al amigo Señor Pez, pajarita

charla de viajes que quiere hacer

por el desierto arenoso

algún amarillo amanecer.

Old lizards whisper *cuentos,*
"*Amigos,* once upon a time,
we drank pitchers of moonlight
long after our bedtime."

Las lagartijas ancianas cuentan,
"Amigos, en un tiempo lejano,
bebimos jarras de luz de luna
sin ir a la cama temprano."

Tonight, young and old
dance to moon and starlight too,
join in the fiesta,
the delicious hullabaloo.

Hoy, jóvenes y viejitos bailan
a la luna y la estrella brillosa
celebrando su fiesta,
la pachanga deliciosa.

Pat Mora is renowned as a writer of poetry, stories for children, and nonfiction. Among her many works are the poetry collections *Borders, Chants,* and *Communion*; the children's books *The Desert Is My Mother/El desierto es mi madre* and *The Gift of the Poinsettia/El regalo de la flor de nochebuena*; and the memoir *House of Houses*. A native of El Paso, she grew up in a bilingual home. Pat Mora has three children and divides her time between Cincinnati and the Southwest.

Renombrada escritora de libros de poesía, cuentos infantiles y ensayos, **Pat Mora** es autora de los poemarios *Chants, Borders,* y *Communion*; de los libros infantiles *El desierto es mi madre/The Desert Is My Mother* y *El regalo de la flor de nochebuena/The Gift of the Poinsettia;* y un libro de memorias *House of Houses.* Nacida y criada en un hogar bilingüe en El Paso, Texas, Pat Mora tiene tres hijos y actualmente divide su residencia entre Cincinnati y el Sudoeste de los Estados Unidos.

Francisco X. Mora divides his time between Mexico and the United States. His many books include *Juan Tuza and the Magic Pouch, The Ballerina Butterfly/La mariposa bailarina, The Little Red Ant and the Great Big Crumb,* and *The Legend of the Two Moons.* He writes: "My brothers and I were born in Mexico City. Every opportunity we had, my family would go to visit relatives in the town of Uruapan, where my grandfather ran a general store. The local marketplace was always filled with people and merchants, wonderful smells, colorful flowers, and exotic fruits. These are the sights and sounds I remember."

Francisco X. Mora divide su residencia entre México y los Estados Unidos. Entre los numerosos libros que ha ilustrado figuran *Juan Tuza and the Magic Pouch, La mariposa bailarina/The Ballerina Butterfly, The Little Red Ant and the Great Big Crumb,* y *The Legend of the Two Moons.* Escribe lo siguiente: "Mis hermanos y yo nacimos en la Ciudad de México, pero nos aprovechamos de cualquier oportunidad de visitar a familiares en Uruapan, donde mi abuelo tenía una tienda de abarrotes. La plaza de mercado siempre se atestaba de gente y de vendedores, y nos envolvían coloridas flores, frutas exóticas y fragancias maravillosas. Estos son los sonidos y las vistas que recuerdo".